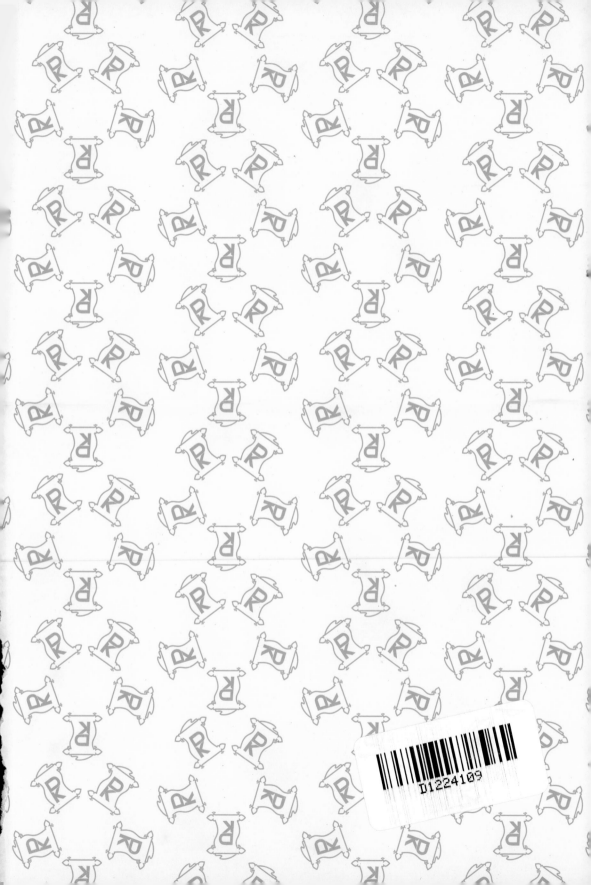

Unique Art of Warli Paintings

To my
precious grandchildren
Ananya, Adwit and Anwita

Unique Art of
Warli Paintings

by

Sudha Satyawadi

D.K. Printworld (P) Ltd.
Publishers of Indian Traditions

Cataloging in Publication Data — DK
[Courtsey: D.K. Agencies (P) Ltd. <docinfo@dkagencies.com>]

Satyawadi, Sudha.
   Unique art of Warli paintings / by Sudha Satyawadi.
      p.   cm.
   Includes bibliographical references (p.   ) and index.
   ISBN 13: 9788124605578
   ISBN 10: 8124605572

   1. Painting, Warli. 2. Folk art — India.   I. Title.

DDC 759.954   22

ISBN 13: 978-81-246-0557-8   **ISBN 10: 81-246-0557-2**
First published in India in 2010
© Author

Published and printed by:
D.K. Printworld (P) Ltd.
Regd. Office: 'Srikunj', F-52, Bali Nagar
Ramesh Nagar Metro Station
New Delhi-110 015
Phones: (011) 2545 3975; 2546 6019; *Fax:* (011) 2546 5926
E-mail: indology@dkprintworld.com
Website: www.dkprintworld.com

Preface

Folk and tribal art have always fascinated me. This art originated in early tribal and agriculture communities containing in itself the thoughts and beliefs of early man. After a long continuous journey through generations it is still popular in villages and is now attracting urban art lovers. Over time, this art came into contact with numerous cultures and has assimilated outside influence, without losing its original character. In early stages this art was associated with religion. As of today, different regions have their own style of painting. Yet there is something common with other styles and some regional peculiarities. All such traditional art has contributed to building the culture of this country.

Warli Art got its name from Warli tribes of Maharashtra. Their art is very close to rock art of central India but with a powerful narrative power. Warli paintings added a new dimension to tribal art. They use brown mud plastered walls of their huts as their canvas, and paint tribal designs in white or brilliant *sindūra* red. Agricultural implements used by them, and areas allotted for rice pounding, worship, marriage etc. are all decorated with typical motifs like trees and creepers, birds and animals, sun and moon, man and woman. Painting is also done on side walls at the entrance of dwellings. Main focus of these drawings is on fertility, averting disease, propitiating the dead, and fulfilling the demands of ghost spirits who fill the dream world of the Warlis.

Warli paintings have seen three stages of evolution. In the first stage, paintings were made on walls on auspicious occasions inside huts and were called *chauk* or *maṇḍala*. Generally, paintings were made at marriages and in harvest season. In the second stage, Warli artists were given paper and colour. They made paintings on rituals, myths, wisdom stories told by ancestors, man's origin and their movement. In the third stage, Warli art became commercial and artists are now making paintings according to the tastes of customers. In this stage the subject of paintings relates to their activities in daily life. This was a parallel development with the traditional one. In the rat race of rapid commercialization this small book is a humble effort to document the traditional art of Warlis.

My thanks to the library staff of Indira Gandhi National Centre for Arts, National Museum, India International Center, College of Arts Pittsburgh University and, Art Library of Ohio State University USA. There is little written material on Warli paintings and their world. Most of the substance for this book, I have collected from Warli artists themselves — my special thanks to all of them especially Sh. Anil Chaitya Wangad of Warli village of Maharashtra. My husband Dr Nitish Satyawadi gave valuable suggestions at every stage in writing of this book. I received constant encouragement from my sons Alok and Amit, daughters-in-law, Reena and Swati. My precious grandchildren Ananya, Adwit and Anwita gazed at Warli paintings around me with genuine curiosity and asked innocent little questions. Credit for including many paintings here goes to them.

Contents

1

Warlis and Their Paintings

Introduction

Warli painting has its own place in the folk art history of India. Paintings are done by village artists and can be seen after every two or three huts in the village. Warli paintings originally adorned mud walls of homes. Paintings are deeply rooted in tradition. Apart from magical belief, a feeling for beautiful form and a sense of colour and proportion — an innate aesthetic drive — leads the artist to decorate his mud hut and also items of daily use.

Warlis use mud plastered walls of huts as their canvas and paint tribal designs in white or brilliant *sindūra* or red colour. Painted with white colour on austere brown surface make it different from other tribal paintings of India. Sometimes red and yellow dots, are supposed to be auspicious, add beauty to the paintings.

Warli paintings represent an artist's relationship with life and everything that is part of it — religion, ritual, livelihood, family, relationship and death. Paintings are an expression of a kind of fulfilment they experience in harmony with nature and their gods and goddesses. Their art is a part of the ritual tradition and exists for a very specific purpose where it fulfils the aims of an individual or a community. Ritual tradition of Warlis is found all over the year with continuous festivities, songs and dance. Making paintings on walls of their huts is at its peak in the marriage season. Every occasion is represented in their art and is connected with their livelihood, their joy and sorrow and related to symbols bearing magical significance. Painted symbols and motifs are repeated on paintings without any change. Paintings convey all that the Warlis feel about their life which was earlier captured in the strict conventions of the *chauk*. It was a constant pressure on Warli painters to make only traditional *chauk*.

Warli art was discovered in early nineteenth century. It was found different from other folk and tribal art of India. This art added a new dimension to tribal art.

In early 1970s Warli artists were supplied brown paper and white paint by the Handicraft and Handloom Board. This led to a startling release of their creative energy in this direction that had so far remained suppressed under tradition and convention. The result was obvious. Warli paintings gained both national and international recognition for this originality of expression. Now, the focus stands changed. Instead of concentrating on gods, paintings depict the day-to-day life of Warli.

There is a shift towards commercialization in the content and form of Warli art that is now based on the appeal of the mass market. This could be a work on sowing, harvesting, cutting wood from tree, dancing in a circle around the *tarpa* player, etc. The pioneer for this change was Jivya Soma Mashe and with him the whole village began to paint on paper. Demand came from outside agencies. The result is that the earlier static forms are being replaced by dynamic and decorative motifs. The traditional *chauk* was replaced by painting of their own experience. This was a parallel development with the traditional one.

To appreciate Warlis' art fully, a little about the Warli people, their religion, their gods and goddesses, their myths and rituals.

Warlis

Warli paintings take their name from Warli tribes of Maharashtra though they are spread out in parts of Gujarat also. Warlis are largely concentrated in the forest area near Dahanu and Talaseri talukas in Thane district. The region lies on the Sahyadri Hills, north of Western Ghats. They were originally nomadic food gathering people of the hills. Later, they took to cultivation growing a single crop, usually paddy, for subsistence or gathering forest

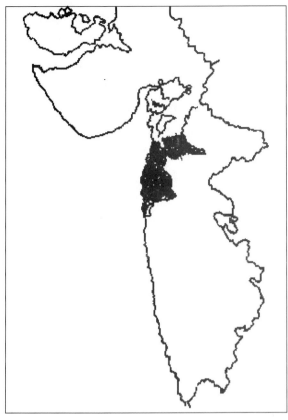

fig. 1. Map of Western Ghat

products and domesticating livestock. Many Warlis state that their ancestors migrated from the north in search of new pastures. The language of the Warlis contains many Sanskrit, Gujarati, Marathi and Hindi words. Assimilation of words from many different languages points to a close association between the Warlis and other people.

A pattern of migration can be traced from the north as indicated by the use of Sanskrit words like *dharatī*, *gāyatrī*, *surā*, *manuj* etc. More revealing are the epic songs, which contain images of a ceaseless conflict between the dark naked Mother Goddess and the gods, notably Indra. And indeed the humiliation of the Mother Goddess is the haunting strain of many of the songs sung during marriage and death. It also forms the central motif in the mythic imagination of the Warlis. (Y. Dalmia, 1962: 64). Besides, it has some similarity with the Haṛappan art and paintings on pottery. The art of the Warlis seems to belong to the phase classified as Neolithic in the rock paintings of central India (3000 BCE to 2500 BCE). (Does this indicate that Warlis once belonged to the north?)

Warlis earn their livelihood by practising agriculture with paddy as their main crop. They have their own social organization in which there is no caste differentiation. Their life is very simple. Many couples live together and have children without getting married. The head of the village is the *sarpañch* who looks after the welfare of the villagers and settles all disputes. Virtual rulers of the community are the *bhagata*s or *raval*s, the priest-cum-medicine men. Nothing can be done without consulting them.

They live in huts that are square in shape, constructed of wooden poles, plastered with mud. Warli hut takes one back to the caves where the first man lived. Huts are completely dark with no windows. At night men and animals sleep together in the hut in complete harmony.

Warlis love to make their environment beautiful. They paint the mud walls of huts with tribal designs in white on *geru* red background. Besides this, everything in their household from the wall of their dwellings to the plough, sieve and flour grinder — is painted with typical motifs like tree and creepers, birds, animals, sun, moon, man and woman. Their paintings

fig. 2. Warli Hut

capture the life around them and throw up a concrete depiction of everyday life of plants, animals and men where even the minutest creature is not forgotten. Paintings are also done on side walls at the entrance of dwellings. For them this should be done — to promote fertility, avert disease, propitiate the dead, fulfil demands of ghost spirits who fill the dream world of the tribal.

fig. 3. Warli Life

Raw materials used for paintings are as simple as their life. Surface for their paintings are the mud walls of huts and the implements, from items of daily use. Wood from forest provides the brush, mud, cow-dung, pounded rice, and *sindūra* are other materials. The surface on which they paint is first cleaned, and smeared with cow-dung. After the dung paste dries up, it receives a *geru* coating. The ground is now ready for painting. Main motifs are palm impressions, footsteps, representation of tree, leaves, stylized drawings of paddy (paddy symbolizes their God), birds, beasts, men and women in geometrical forms. Recently added motifs like motor car, train and

fig. 4. Warli Life

fig. 5. Warli Life

fig. 6. Warli Life

fig. 7. Warli Life

fig. 8. Warli Life

bicycles are frequently used by artists. Impact of industrialization has left its permanent imprint on tribals.

Bhagatas or Ravals

Religious worship is not possible without the mediation of a *bhagata* or priest. The *bhagatas*, also called *ravals*, are vested with all knowledge of the gods and it is in their power to propitiate or scare away a deity. To get a bhagatahood, one has to undergo a very serious training under a senior *bhagata*. The training is carried out in secrecy. In earlier times *bhagatas* took their training in caves called *vairgi* — house of the Mother Earth. Any special or difficult training which has to be imparted in great secrecy is undertaken in these caves. Four or five camps have to be attended for completing ravalhood. After these camps, students have to undergo special training with the recognized *bhagata*.

fig. 9. Training of Bhagatahood

This painting (*fig.* 9) made by Balu Dumara depicts the training of bhagatahood. In the painting *a raval* is seated in the centre with the chief *bhagata* sitting under the shed near a fire. The students are holding a whip to beat themselves with. On the right some *bhagata*s are running after witches (shown with flying hair) with whips. The training of bhagatahood is forbidden to women because they become witches and misuse the knowledge. They seem to appear stronger than the *bhagata*s who are chasing them. In the left, a witch is riding on a dog because that is what would bring them with speed to go where the *bhagata* is. Another witch sits on a bundle of grass for she comes like the wind. The painting depicts the extreme paranoia that *bhagatas* feel about the witches.

2

Religious Beliefs

Gods and Goddesses

Gods live through the hearts of a believing people. They have no existence apart from this. The chief gods are the elements of nature. Besides Mother Goddess, sun and moon gods, they have the god of thunder, of lightning, of great wind, of rain, and many others. When crops become ripe, the household gods Hirva, Himai, Jhotinga and Nārāyaṇdeva are worshipped. During harvest, Cheda or the village guardians are worshipped for protection of the fields. Offerings are made to tiger god Bāghdeva and the guardian of every three villages. This takes place at the festival of Kansari, the goddess. Then comes the wedding season with celebration of marriages. The main gods and goddesses of Warlis are:

> Kansari, the Great Mother
> Nārāyaṇdeva
> Bāghadeva
> Hirva
> Cheda
> Kṣetrapālas / Ancestor God
> Sun
> Moon

Mahalakṣmī the Great Mother

The life of Warlis is centred around the cult of Mother Goddess. According to them, their chief goddess is *ai* or the mother who looks after their welfare. She is worshipped in the form of Dhanvantarī, Mother Earth, Gavatari, the Mother Cow, and Kansari, the goddess of corn, Pālaghāṭ, the plants and

fig. 10. Goddess Mahalakshmi Temple

goddess of marriage. In the cult of the Mother Goddess women are vested with especially creative powers since it is they who give birth to life. The belief in the mother leads to the cyclic year, where each year is born, attains maturity and dies in summer when the paddy is cut. The whole wonder of life, marriage and death is symbolized by the cult of the Mother and is given concrete expression in the form of rituals.

Kansari

The goddess of corn, Kansari is propitiated when the paddy has been cut. Goddess Kansari takes the dominant place in the harvest festival, for without her, the fields would be barren. She is always seen riding a tiger. Her body is formed of leaf and merges with the stripes of the tiger. In many rituals, Warlis refer to the Great Mother as in the song of Kansari or the *bhagata's* song during the wedding in the presence of the goddess Pālaghāṭ, looming large in the painting. The song of Kansari sung during this time narrates the story of the goddess of corn. In the Kansari song there is continuous struggle between the primitive earth goddess and gods which could only belong to the age when Indra was an important god, i.e. in early Vedic period. All this points to an all-pervasive cult of the Mother Goddess which exercises considerable influence to this day.

Pālaghāṭ

The bountiful nature is personified in the form of Pālaghāṭ, the goddess of trees and plants who presides over a marriage. Acutely aware of the primeval processes of birth and death, the Warlis believe that these are contained within the very womb of the Mother. The overflowing pot with vegetation symbolizes the goddess. Formed by two triangles — one pointing

fig. 11. Goddess Pālaghāṭ

upwards and representing the male element, *pāla* — the erect stone — and the other pointing downwards and symbolizing the female principle, the *ghāṭ* — the embodiment of all creative energy — the form is creation itself. The Warlis, while delineating the sacred form, are careful to see that the lines of the two triangles do not intersect, for it is this characteristic that distinguishes divinity from man. (Pupal Jaykar, 1980: 174). Human form is depicted by intersecting triangles. The goddess is enshrined in a richly ornamented square *maṇḍala*.

Pañca Sūryadeva

Pañca Sūryadeva is generally drawn adjacent to the goddess Pālaghāṭ in marriage *maṇḍala*. The five headed god is encased within a square *maṇḍala*. Horses in a row are also drawn on the wall near the marriage *maṇḍala*.

fig. 12. Panca Sūryadeva

Gavatari

Gavatari the goddess of cow is worshipped at the time of Diwālī till the *pūjā* of the tiger god. After that Warli cannot play *tarpa*. In Holī they play only the drum and dance.

Himai

Himai is the mother of mountains and supervises over cattle and sheep. She is shown seated on a tiger and is one aspect of Goddess Earth.

Pānadeva

Pānadeva is the god of vegetation and the wedding symbolizes the union of the vegetation and goddess.

Nārāyaṇdeva

With the coming of the first grains of rice, the festival of Nārāyaṇdeva, the god of rain, is celebrated with *kamdi* dance.

Bāghadeva/God of Tiger

All tribes share the common religious awe of the tiger god Bāghadev. He is the guardian of every three villages and is worshipped. Offerings are made to him. In paintings, Bāghadeva can be painted in his benevolent and in ferocious forms in the same painting. Tiger god has to be propitiated before the worship of the Mother Goddess Kansari. Festival of Bāghadeva takes place in the month of Kārtika (November). The entire festival takes place over three days and nights in which *bhagata*s invoke the spirit of the god.

The painting (*fig.* 13) depicts *bhagata*s seated in front of the tiger god and preparing for the ritual. *Utare bhagata*s evoke the spirit of the god. The *dak bhagata*s sit with the *daks* and *tandula bhagata*s who are performing the ritual looking at the *tandula* (rice). The *bhagata*s are more in number because the chanting becomes easier. Next to *bhagata*s sit a circle of people drinking toddy and next to them a group of figures are dancing to the *tarpa*. On the side of Bāghadeva band players are playing music. A goat is taken for the ceremony and sacrifice. Other scenes depict the day-to-day life of Warlis.

fig. 13. Bāghadeva

fig. 14. Ancestor's Worship

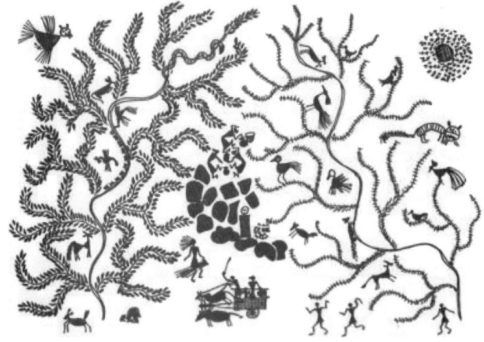

Vīras — Ancestor God or Village Guardians

The household gods protect Warlis in their homes. Main village deities worshipped are associated with the heroic cult of fertilizing and protecting the *kṣetra*. Their fields are looked after by the *vīras* or the heroic ancestor gods. The dead ancestors ward off evil spirits and dangerous animals from the fields. In this sense the *vīras* are known as *kṣetrapālas*. In their paintings they weave tangible reality with fantasy in the form of ancestor god. Hirva, a prominent god, is represented by Jhotiṅga and, other gods' original forms are *liṅgas* found in small villages.

Cheda God

The most developed and chief ancestor is the Cheda to protect the Warlis from danger. When they go to some distant place they always remember Cheda to protect them and help them in sorting out difficulties. No one leaves his house without remembering him.

Hirva

Hirva represents the fecund, fertile aspects of nature. He is just as important as Śiva. Warlis believe that Hirva is more fiery than other gods and is quick to bring illness to the family if not constantly propitiated. Hirva is represented as a bunch of peacock feathers stuck into a bamboo stick and to be kept at the place of worship. The bamboo stick is known as Jhotiṅga, Hirva's protection.

Jortiba

Jortiba derives from plough and is a prominent *kṣetrapāla* god. Four handed Jortiba rides a horse or a snake, holding in his two left hands a *triśula* (spear), and *pānapātra* (liquor vessel) and on his two right hands *ḍamarū* (drum), and *khaḍga* (sword).

3

Rites and Rituals

Cosmic Change of Season

As season follows season, nature changes its form. The god appropriate to each season is worshipped as season changes. The agricultural season for Warlis begins around Vaiśākhi (May). At the harvesting of the first rice crop the festival of Nārāyaṇdeva, God of Rain is worshipped with *kamdi* dance and festivities.

fig. 15. Beginning of Season

In this painting harvest has begun. Grain is threshed, the year's supply stored and the new rice is ready to be eaten. Warlis celebrate the event with a formal ceremony. Neighbours are summoned with the blowing of a *tarpa*, the Warli's pipe. It is an invitation to the celebration. An old man dances round a pole crowned by a flame. At the base of the pole are baskets, full of the new grain, the first of the season, nature's gift to the community.

Harvest

When crops become ripe, the household gods, Hirva, Himai, Jortiba and Nārāyaṇdeva are worshipped and placed in the attic above the kitchen. During harvest Cheda or the village guardian is worshipped for only he can protect their field. In the month of Bhādrapada (September) people begin harvesting with the worship of Sāvanī, the goddess of the field. A *pūjā* is performed so that the harvest is plentiful and no injury is caused to the people while cutting the crop. Before the festival, offerings are made to Bāghadeva.

Following this at the end of Āśvini (October), when the rice crop has ripened, the festival of the corn goddess Kansari is celebrated. At Dīwālī, festivities reach a climax. On Dīwālī, the festival of lights, as the lamps are lit and fire crackers go off, the *tarpa*, the Warli pipe is used to summon young couples of the village to dance in a ring. It is a merry go round of light, sound and festivity.

fig. 16. Bāghadeva (from fig. 13)

fig. 17. Diwali Festivities

During the festivities, a goat or a chicken is sacrificed to the god concerned and then distributed and eaten by those present. This is followed by a dance which culminates in their being possessed.

Marriage (Warli Wedding)

Then comes the marriage season. The presiding deity of marriage is goddess Pālaghāṭ. The *bhagatas* are taken over by gods. The song of creation conjures up images of cosmic cycle of creation, destruction and re-creation. The seasonal circle then ends and there is a fresh beginning. The cycle is best represented by a circle, which has neither an end nor a beginning and is usually made at the place where grain is pounded.

Warli marriage season usually starts from Māgha (February) to Phālguna (March) with festivities, dance and song. This is also the culmination of the ritual cycle of a year. It is only when crops have been stored, the Warlis savour the fruits of their labour by celebrating individual marriage which takes place over three days. The presiding deity of marriage Pālaghāṭ, the vegetation goddess, is worshipped. They also worship other gods with song and dance. Each wedding after the harvest is seen as one which will bring about the union of the universe and the bride and bridegroom are seen as a divine couple coming together.

When a boy and a girl decide to marry, the boy pays the price for the bride depending on the financial condition of the boy's family. A boy can marry four or five girls but the girl is not allowed to marry more then one boy. But a girl can leave her man asserting her will to be free.The chosen man has to pay the bride price to her husband. The maternal uncle is important in many rites and rituals in marriage. Generally weddings take place after harvest. Marriage ceremony takes three days. *Maṇḍapa*s are constructed at boy's place and paintings are made in the hut, in the kitchen and near the rice hole. *Bhagata* plays an important role in marriage rites. The first day ceremony of *maṇḍapa bandhane* is performed at boy's place. In this ceremony a *maṇḍapa*, a rough wooden pavilion, is constructed outside the hut and simultaneously a drawing of a fertility goddess is made on a side wall of the hut. The dark hut of Warlis provides a good location for wedding paintings. They stand out in darkest recesses of hut in their sparkling white outline of rice flour. The *bhagata* would sing songs of the god Hirva. And when he has reached a state of being in trance, he uncovers the marriage paintings. Only then it is considered animated with life. Most wedding ceremonies are still performed by the *bhagata*. In songs of marriage, as the auspicious moment nears, in order to ward off evil spirits, the Warlis remember the whole galaxy of gods.

It is on the next day, wearing ceremonial headbands, the tribal couple leave for their new house.

Ritual of Death

The religious beliefs of the Warlis can be seen in their mythic knowledge of death. Death is not the end of human existence. It is but another beginning. In both death and marriage almost similar rites are observed. In the case of a couple whose marriage has not been solemnized in their lifetime, at the time of the death of one person, the other is considered finally married to him. The dead can again be born in the form of their grandchildren. No cremation takes place of the young who are mostly buried. Jum, the god of death, takes him away and he is made to work according to his past deeds.

For five days after death, the spirit of the dead does not leave the house, but stays quite close to the wall and watches if the rites are performed in a proper way. The rites, *divas*, has to be performed as soon as possible. In songs related to death they not only worship the sun, moon gods, but also the gods of lightning, god of happiness, god of thunder and rain god of pillar and the god of thin wire.

Rites, rituals and festivities lend colour, meaning and even significance to life. Here are the few ways in which Warlis punctuate the daily business of living with celebrations. It is a ritual to give offerings to *jungle dev* as depicted in this painting.

4

Warli Paintings

I. Three Stages of Warli Paintings

Tribal paintings of Warlis resemble Neolithic rock paintings of central India. They are characterized by white outlines, triangular human and animal figures with geometrical designs. Warli paintings have seen three stages of its evolution. In the first stage paintings were made on walls on auspicious occasions inside huts and called *chauk* or *maṇḍala*. In the second stage artists were given paper and colour and they made paintings on rituals, myths, wisdom stories told by ancestors, man's origin and their movement. This was the period when painters tried to immortalize their culture, rituals and ideas and their height of fantasy. In the third stage Warli art became commercial and artists are now making paintings according to the tastes of their customers. In this stage subjects of the paintings are mainly their activities in daily life.

Paintings were made in marriages and harvest season and other auspicious occasions but marriage *chauk*s are more popular. Warlis feel they are essential, for without these marriage cannot take place. Even today the Warlis are continuing this tradition. They never do anything without significance. Rites, rituals and festivities lend colour, meaning and even significance to life. Ritual paintings are also known as *chauk*. Warlis are continuing this tradition. For *chauk* Warlis say:

> *Chauk lit age kaya ge riti,*
> *Chauk lit age raya re riti*

(What is the reason of writing a *chauk*, we are drawing because it is a convention.)

First Stage — Wedding Paintings

A Warli marriage calls for a special wall painting. This shows the participation of the entire universe in human form. Generally marriage *chauk*s are made on the wall of their huts. The artists of these paintings are *suvasini*s which means married women whose husbands are alive.

From early morning they start and by dusk the whole painting is to be finished. This is on the day of wedding. The picture is drawn in secrecy and kept veiled, a mystery to be revealed only at the auspicious hour. The goddess of vegetation Goddess Pālaghāṭ presides over the ceremonies. *Suvasini*s prepare wall for painting by cleaning the wall with cow-dung.

When dung paste is dry the surface is smeared with *geru* (red mud) and rice paste is prepared for painting. Two *suvasini*s first make a marriage painting which is known as *chauk*. The painting

fig. 18. Preparation of Marriage Chauk

depicts the marriage ceremony, with the vegetable goddess Pālaghāṭ in the centre, her guardian Pañca Sūryadeva on the side surrounded by landscape in which the wedding is taking place. The figure of fertility goddess is made with the hands and feet spread apart in the position of giving birth to a child. She is framed in a square with geometrical designs. Inside the *chauk* the cosmos come to life with the images of sun and moon. Animals in the paintings, though said to be a horse, resemble a bull rather than a horse. All the carrying, riding and ploughing was done by oxen-shaped animals. There is considerable difference in form and content between one region and another.

fig. 19. Marriage Maṇḍala

In each painting one finds figure of Goddess Pālaghāṭ in the centre and the landscape of animals, trees, and humans bear a close relationship to each other. The entire painting with its richly textured symbols is the only ornamentation in the Life of Warlis. When two women are working together on a big *chauk* simultaneously other women draw two smaller *chauks* on both sides and show five headed god Pañca Sūryadeva on a horseback in the middle. The tree, animals and men and women engaged in some activity are also drawn in empty space outside the *chauk*. Pānadeva is the god of vegetation and the wedding symbolizes the union of vegetation and the goddess.

All bountiful nature is personified in the form of Pālaghāṭ goddess of tree and plants, who presides as without her a marriage cannot take place. She is also the provider of children. Goddess Pālaghāṭ is symbolized as pot or *ghaṭa* symbol of womb overflowing with plants. Other paintings are placed on the kitchen wall, a small partitioned square in the hut. It is the darkest part in the hut and a woman's place where she spends most of her time. In front of the painting is always a rice hole or *ukhaal*.

The main painting is drawn in secrecy and kept veiled. The mystery is to be revealed only at the auspicious hour. Three holy men arrive singing. One of them chosen by others for his special powers, waits for the divine spirit to enter his body. In this state of trance his perceptions are highlighted in the coming event, he tears the veil down and names the bride.

CIRCLE

At the time of the wedding, *suvasinis* draw white concentric circles (filled with dots) *bhavara*, inside the *maṇḍapa* near the entrance of the hut, on the floor, and two on rice hole *ukhāl*. At the time of marriage a circular *raṅgolī bhavara* is drawn and the groom and the bride stand on it which is supposed to be auspicious.

Circles are also related to death. These patterns are drawn at funeral rites. Warlis say that *pala* trees grow in these circles. After a person dies his body is taken out of the house to a far off place which is surrounded by lots of trees. At the time of birth these circles are drawn and filled with dots as a symbol of the birth of goddess Sathi.

Second Stage

In the second stage the Warli artists were given paper and colours and they made paintings on their rituals, myths, wisdom stories told by ancestors, man's origin and their movements. Best paintings are made in this period. Their unique narrative power made these paintings very popular.

In 1970s and 1980s some Warli artists translated on paper what they made on the hut walls. Jivya Soma Mase was first among them and was the most successful of Warli artists who paint on paper. He gave a new look to the *chauk* paintings of the Warli. He is rooted in his tradition and at the same time rises above it to give expression to his personal world of art which is unique. His favourite subject is Mother Goddess Pālaghāṭ and other goddesses in different forms and the seasonal depiction of the festival of Nārāyaṇdeva, which takes place during harvest.

Many of the myths and legends of the Warlis centred round the bountiful corn goddess Kansari and was worshipped to bloom their fields. When she feels neglected she walks away with anger allowing people to starve. The paintings depict how the life on earth was created by Śiva and Pārvatī and proliferated on earth. How the first man died, life and death are both contained within the womb of the earth, arising from the same mysterious source and sustained by it.

Balu Dumara is another Warli artist. Both these artists focused on myths and legends related to gods, and various phenomena of nature, i.e. flora and fauna, are recorded and presented through their paintings. Such paintings are referred to as 'narrative paintings' as they depict their myths, legends and associated grandmother tales.

Third Stage

In the third stage the earlier static of forms is being replaced by dynamic and decorative symbols. Warli art became commercial and artists are making paintings according to the tastes of their customers. In this stage subjects of the paintings mainly depict their observations of everyday life. Warlis live a very simple life. Their huts are square, the floor bare and few belongings can be seen hanging from the walls like sickle (used to chop food for cooking), a small tobacco basket, dried vegetables and *tarpa*, their musical instrument, in the paintings. A small square portion is their kitchen and a narrow strip is separated by a low fence, for the cattle. At night, men and cattle sleep together in the hut in comfortable closeness. Their paintings are a concrete depiction of everyday life and activities, of plants, animals and men where even the minute creature is not forgotten. Trees have an important place in the Warli paintings because they have always lived amidst them. A variety of trees in the painting creates a feeling of abundance and well being.

II. Myths and Legends

The song of creation conjures up images of the cosmic cycle of creation, destruction and re-creation. It begins with the creation of elemental gods like the moon, sun, god of clouds, and others and goes on to destroy this world.

Yet another aeonic cycle of time begins with the sowing of seeds from which emerges the whole of beginning of creation with vegetation and going on to human and animals. The seasonal cycle ends as it begins. With their natural instinct for ecology, however, Warlis realize that there cannot be endless creation and so death enters to lighten Mother Earth's burden. Thus begins another circle of creation and destruction reminding us of the grandiose structure devised by gods.

For the Warli, life is an ever renewing source of wonder and bounty which they tell us through their stories. Their tales tell us how the earth was created by Śiva and Pārvatī, how the first man died and so on. Life and death are both contained within the womb of the earth, arising from the same mysterious source and sustained by it. Many of the myths and legends of the Warlis centred round the bountiful goddess of corn, goddess Kansari and worship her to bloom their fields. Gods live in the heart of the believing people. They have no existence apart from this. And what is more, they are very nearly human. Sometimes God teaches a lesson to people and other gods when they take every thing easy. When God feels neglected he walks away with anger allowing people to starve.

The original self-created couple are Mahādeva and Gaṅgā Gaurī and life on earth was created by them. They created the universe. Mahādeva created many gods like the Sun, Moon, god of Lightning, god of Thunder and the god of Clouds. This original self-created couple who set about sowing seeds obtained from squirrels and ants. After they finished their work, life began to proliferate on earth.

A myth says that Mahādeva and Gaurī looked down from the heavens and found the earth bare of trees. They descended, armed with bags of seeds. Mahādeva setoff in one direction and Gaurī in the other, planting seeds along the way. They walked for many years, covering the parched brown earth with lush green trees.

Beginnings of Vegetation

Gaurī grew old and grey, Mahādeva lean and weary. Thus they met, their bags empty of grain, their good deed done. "Who are you?" asked Mahādeva as he met an old woman hobbling along. "I am Gaurī," replied the woman. "And I am your husband, Mahādeva. Our work is done, let us go home." After they had finished their work, life began to proliferate on earth.

Another myth says once upon a time the Warlis were blessed with plentiful harvests. There was no famine for years. Then, one day, the lord of harvests decided to see for himself how grateful his people were for the blessings they received at his hands.

Wrath of Gods

The lord took the form of a cat and went to a house just as the family

fig. 20. Beginning of Vegetation

members were about to sit down to a meal. "Chase that thief of a cat away," they cried. He went to another house, this time disguised as a dog. It was the same. "We can't have dogs prowling around begging for food." The lord of harvest tried again. This time he appeared at a house disguised as a holy man. "We are sorry. We have nothing left to offer you." The lord walked away, seething with anger. All the granaries were soon empty as the grain grew legs and followed their lord out of the land of the Warlis. This is why, or so the Warlis believe, their bins have never been full again.

Lightning flashed and thunder rumbled as clouds raced across the sky in readiness for the annual assembly of the weather gods. They met, and waited eagerly for Mahādeva, the Great God, to arrive. As the appointed hour approached, Mahādeva decided to test both their devotion to him, and their wisdom. He appeared before them clothed in tiger skin and covered with

fig. 21. Wrath of Gods

buzzing flies. "Go away. This is an assembly of the gods." "We are waiting for Mahādeva. Stop fouling the air with your filthy garments." And they pushed him out.

Lesson to Gods

Mahādeva went straight to his wife Gaurī. "I will be away for a long time. My fellow gods need to be taught a lesson in humility. There will be drought in the land. Fill your water pot, and don't breathe a word to anybody" and he went away. The gods waited for twelve long years. They grew lean and hungry and thirsty, for no food or water would they touch while waiting for Mahādeva. At last they set out to look for him. They found him across a huge expanse of water. "Where have you been Mahādeva? Had you forgotten about our assembly?" Mahādeva answered calmly, "I came, but you pushed me away. So I left you in anger." "That old man?" "That half-mad beggar?"

fig. 22. Lesson to Gods

asked gods. "Yes" said Mahādeva. If you had taken the trouble to look closer, you would have recognized me. I hope you have learnt your lesson. Here, you may drink this rice water."

The water was stale and filled with wriggling worms. The gods, not daring to refuse, drank. And as they drank they realized with relief that the worms were only reflections of their own tangled and overgrown beards! Mahādeva returned with them. Lightning flashed once more, thunder rumbled and rain clouds poured their bounty on the parched and waiting earth.

Once, Mahādeva the Great God, invited Lord Nārāyaṇdeva to eat with him. He arranged for the best chickens to be cooked for the meal. It was a lavish feast. The next day he wanted to find out how Nārāyaṇdeva had liked the food.

Feast for Gods

He disguised himself as a herdsman and went to him. "How did you like the food that Mahādeva served you?" asked Mahādeva. Nārāyaṇdeva replied, "Oh, it was all right. Nothing special, just a bit of chicken." Mahādeva was disappointed. He decided to make another attempt to please Nārāyaṇdeva. "This time I will serve him a whole goat." After the feast, the herdsman again appeared before Nārāyaṇdeva. "I hear you were invited again. Did Mahādeva serve you better food this time?" "O nothing very much, just some mutton," replied Nārāyaṇdeva.

Mahādeva was irritated. "I'll serve him what he deserves. I'll give him really humble fare. A dish of land crabs, fit for the poorest of the poor. That will teach him to appreciate a delicacy when he gets it." As usual the herdsman appeared and asked shyly, "What did Mahadev feed you this time? I am sure you liked the food." Nārāyaṇdeva's eyes lit up with joy. "It was a real feast. Juicy land crabs, cooked just right. I could not stop eating."

How Warli got the Names

The Warlis talk of a great deluge that wiped out villages and scattered

fig. 23. Feast to Gods

people. People had to begin their life all over again. A painting depicts how different names have been given to Warli people. New surnames were given according to where, with what or whom, and in what condition people were found after the floodwater receded.

The Wagat ancestor had taken shelter in the cave of a tiger *wag*. The Sabar ancestor was found near a prickly bush *sabar*. The Wangad ancestor floated safely to a place surrounded by *wangi*. The Hand was to get this name because their forefathers were found among pots, i.e. *handa*s. The Kurades clung on to a drifting axe *kurad*. The Pasares chanced to be a group of five *pas* and the Goveres were spotted with a herd of cattle. One of them was with a stack of leaves *pal* and his family on stony *dogar* ground and the Bhavars were washed up near a comb of bees *bhural*. But best of all are the Thackerays whose ancestor slept through it all, left to lie *thakha* undisturbed.

fig. 24. How Warlis got their names

fig. 25. Harvesting

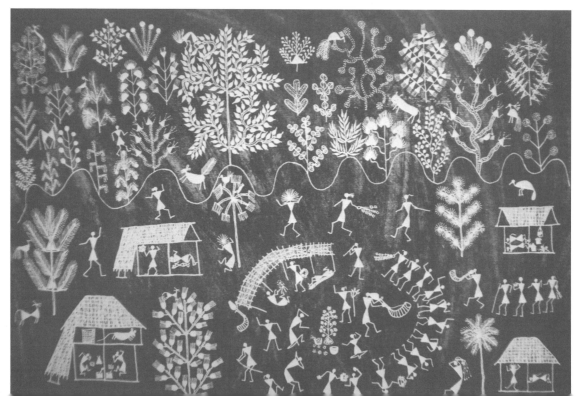

Harvest

Once upon a time the Warlis were blessed with plentiful harvests. There was no famine for years. Then, one day, the lord of harvests decided to see for himself how grateful his people were for the blessings they received at his hands.

The lord took the form of a cat and went to a house just as the family members were about to sit down to a meal. "Chase that thief of a cat away," they cried. He went to another house, this time disguised as a dog. It was the same. "We can't have dogs prowling around begging for food." The lord of harvest tried again. This time he appeared at a house disguised as a holy man. "We are sorry. We have nothing left to offer you." The lord walked away, seething with anger. All the granaries were soon empty as the grain grew legs and followed their lord out of the land of the Warlis. This is why, or so the Warlis believe, their bins have never been full again.

Spirit of the Forest

Once there was bright sunny afternoon. Two men set out through the jungle to collect honey; for the combs were full and dripping, as they nested in the hollows of the rock. The distant hum of bees drew their attention. "There's a huge honeycomb," said one, pointing at the rock-face in front of them. "Its going to be stiff, but it will be worth it" replied his friend.

They brought the honeycomb down and were soon on their way back. "We forgot to leave behind a few drops as an offering to the jungle spirit. You know that is always done." "I didn't forget," said his friend. "After all, we did all the hard work. Why should the jungle spirit be given a share?" The spirit hovering round, decided to teach them a lesson. He snatched away the comb and drank up all the honey. "Someone has taken our honeycomb." "It is worse. I am being bitten." " And me too. Let us run." Said his friend.

And they took to their heels with the spirit chasing them. It was a lesson for the whole village. Ever since, the first offering of honey is always made to the jungle spirit.

fig. 26. Spirit of the forest

fig. 27. Mahalakshmi Temple

fig. 28. Migration of Warlis

fig. 29. Worship of Ancestors

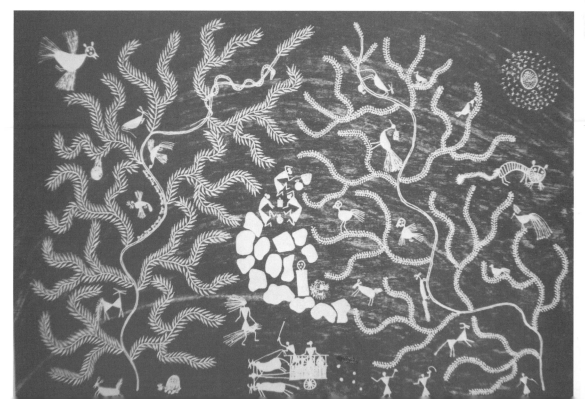

fig. 30. Rejoicing at Diwali

III. Narrative Paintings

Here are some grandma's stories collected from the paintings of Jivya Soma Mashe and Balu Dumara paintings. Their stories tell us how the earth was created by Śiva and Pārvatī, how the first man died and so on. Life is an ever-renewing source of and bounty which they tell us through their stories. Folk wisdom and common sense are quite often represented through animal stories. For, animal ways lend themselves naturally to wit and humour and pure fun. These stories show how Warlis respond to universal human situations in their own inimitable way.

Stories

SEVEN SISTERS AND CRAB

A man had seven daughters. One day he was out in the forest collecting leaves. He had piled up a huge heap and wanted help to lift it. He called out

fig. 32. Unfaithful wife

fig. 33. Life without work

fig. 31. Seven sisters and a crab

for help but no one came forward to give him a hand. He called out again offering one of his daughters in marriage.

A crab crawled up to help him hoist the burden on to his shoulder. The man took the crab home with him and said to his daughters, "There is a crab who helped me in the forest. I promised that one of you would marry him." The girls were amused and poked fun at the crab. "People don't marry crabs. They eat them." The crab was adamant. "I insist on getting my reward." Upon this the youngest girl agreed to marry him, and followed the crab home.

When they arrived at the crab's hole. the crab asked the girl to come in. "Put your head in and I will pull you through," said the crab but the girl hesitated. Suddenly she found herself in a spacious mansion. "I am not really a crab," said her husband as she watched him turn into a handsome young man. The girl was happy and said, "We must go home and give this good news to my father." They went to visit their people the next day. "We don't believe you" said her sisters. "You have left the poor crab and run away with this man. Don't imagine you can fool us." "I am indeed the crab she married," said her husband. "Here is the proof that she speaks the truth," and he changed into a crab right in front of them. As they stood astonished he transformed himself into a man again and walked away with his wife.

UNFAITHFUL WIFE

A newly married woman would not go to her husband. She had a lover. All the villagers knew and some of them were determined to catch her and make her mend her ways. As dusk turned to night she slipped out and was on her way to meet her lover. The watchful villagers stopped her. One of them threw a garland of itchy nettles round her neck. "Your place is by your husband. We shall see that you have a change of heart." As she itched and squirmed they pleaded with her, trying to make her see sense. At length, torn by the guilt and unable to bear her garland of nettles, she repented "I will do as you say. I will go to my husband." They freed her and led her home.

LIFE WITHOUT WORK

There was an old couple in a village. The man was very lazy. While others worked he could usually be found lying around and his wife had to go out into the forest to dig for roots and bring food for him. She nagged him constantly. His only reply was, "God provides me with all I need."

One day while digging in the forest his wife found a pot full of gold and silver. She came running to her husband for help to dig up the pot. As usual he replied, "God will bring it to me." The old woman lost her patience and scolded him so loudly that the other villagers overheard. They hurried to the spot only to find the pot full of snakes and worms. They felt cheated and angry. So they decided to empty it over the old man. To their surprise, when they overturned the pot, out flowed shower of gold and silver coins.

PEACE AND PLENTY

When Warlis pray to the God for peace and tranquility they perform a ritual to honour Lord Nārāyaṇdev. They worship the marigold in full bloom and make an offering of five coconuts and a chicken.

They hide the chicken and coconut in the forest. As people dance around a specially erected canopy, one of them feels the divine spirit entering him and he goes into a trance. At this time bystanders strike him with a bunch of betel nuts strung on fibre ropes. If the man is genuinely possessed he does not feel it, if he is only pretending he cries with the pain.

The chosen one then goes running into the forest, finds the hidden offerings (five coconuts and chicken) and claims them as his own. This way they please Nārāyaṇdev. Each home in turn performs this ritual.

fig. 34. Peace and plenty

MONEY LENDER BECOMES WEALTHY

It was the first seed of grain on its journey down to earth. Somewhere along the way it got changed into a bent old woman, covered with boils and sores from head to foot. The old woman arrived on earth and spent the whole day going from door to door, asking for food, seeking shelter. Every house turned her away. It was nightfall when she reached a moneylender's house. The moneylender took pity on her and let her use his courtyard for the night. In the morning she was gone. To this day the tribal suffer for the hard-heartedness of their forefathers. And to this day the moneylender thrives, rewarded for his act of mercy.

fig. 35. Moneylender becomes wealthy

FARMERS AND THE GHOSTS

A farmer went fishing at night. Returning, he had to walk through the woods. Suddenly there was a rustle of leaves and two ghosts stood before him. "No one walks through these woods at night," said one shadow figure. "We are going to eat you, foolish man," said the other. The man put up a brave front. "Of course you can eat me. But there is something you have to do before my flesh becomes tasty and fit to eat. You have to solve this knotty problem first." Saying this he handed them two puzzles made out of interlocked blades of grass. "You have to take these apart without breaking the blades of grass." The ghosts got busy with the puzzle that they did not notice the sky lighting up. They did not realize that the night would soon be over. As day broke over the hills, the ghosts vanished and the farmer went home, safe and sound.

fig. 36. Farmers and the ghosts

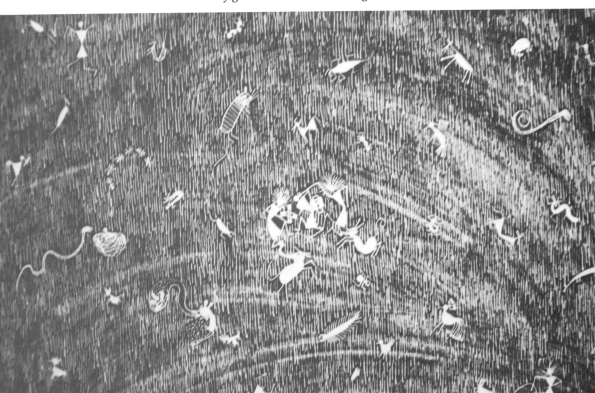

fig. 37. Hermit's daughter

HERMIT'S DAUGHTER

A hermit adopted a little child as his own daughter. She grew up to be a beautiful girl and all the village lads wanted to marry her. But the hermit did not want to part with her. So he laid down almost impossible conditions for her marriage.

In the village square there was a tree full of fruits. It was a place where villagers always gathered to chat or gossip or just lie down beneath it in the shade. Children used to play here and climb in and out of its sturdy branches. The hermit's condition was that any suitor who succeeded in plucking the fruit from the tree without being seen by anyone could have the girl.

A poor widow's son had fallen in love with this girl. He used to sit under a tree all day dreaming of her. One day he had fallen asleep when he woke up to hear the frightened chirping of cranes. He turned around and saw a serpent sliding into the nest of the cranes. He killed the snake and went back to sleep.

When the mother crane returned to feed her young ones, they refused to eat and said, "We will not eat till you ask our father to find out what troubles this young man who saved our life." They told their mother how this man had killed the snake and saved their lives.

The father bird spoke to the young man who told him about the hermit's daughter. "I have a suggestion. Climb on my back and let us go to the riverbed. I will tell you my plan on the way." They collected some sand and flew back to the tree. "As we approach the fruit tree make a lot of noise. The people who are under the tree will look up. Throw a handful of sand over them. While they go groping and rubbing their eyes, quickly pluck some fruits. Nobody will be able to say that they saw you doing it" said the crane. The plan succeeded and the boy married the hermit's daughter. They lived happily ever after.

CRADLE THAT WALKED AWAY

A couple went into the jungle to gather leaves. They had their small baby with them. His wife looked around for a spot where she could put up a hammock. She soon found a pair of convenient branches. She slung her hammock across, rocked her baby to sleep and went about her work.

As they sat down for their midday meal, the husband turned to his wife, "Just look at that! That is a python gliding away, bearing aloft our baby, hammock and all." The wife ran to retrieve her infant who was sleeping soundly through all the confusion. As she came back, clutching the baby, she cried out, "What seem to me like two branches were the antlers of a deer that the python had swallowed whole. What a narrow escape!

MAGIC BOWL

There was a rich man in the village. All villagers would work for him in the field. The poorest among them was a man with hundred children. What he

fig. 38. Cradle that walked away

fig. 39. Magic bowl

was getting as daily wages was not enough for his family. His wife would greet him angrily," Is that all? Why don't you tell your miser master that you have a large family." The poor man asked for more money but he was not showed any mercy and was told, "You do the same work as others so you are paid the same."

His children grew hungrier day by day and his wife angrier. She always accused him for not caring for his family. He could not bear it. Finally he retreated into the jungle. Jungle's strange sounds seemed kinder to him than the nagging of his wife.

One day lord Mahādeva and his wife Gaurī, passing by, saw the poor man in distress. She asked, "You looked troubled. Tell us about it." He told them all. They felt sorry for him and gave him a pot and said," Take this bowl and pass it over your cooking pots. You will have enough rice and lentils for all your family." The poor man returned to his house with this bowl. He again started working for the rich man. Now his life was comfortable.

As time passed the rich man became curious, "These days you do not complain. Why are you so content" he asked. The poor man told the whole story about his meeting with Mahādeva and said, "Come to my house and see for yourself." After seeing all this, the rich man too went into the forest and was seen by Mahādva and Gaurī. "He seems worried" says Gaurī. "Let him be" said Mahādeva in his infinite wisdom. But Gaurī persisted so Mahadeva gave him a bowl also.

The rich man returned home. He thought, "I will invite all the villagers to a meal. That should impress everyone." The villagers were surprised to get this invitation. "The old miser is giving us a meal. We must all go." All went to the rich man's house. He welcomed all, "let the women be fed first" ordered the host. But when his servants passed it over the pots, instead of food out leapt barbers holding razors. There was panic. The women screamed for help. Outside, the men were alarmed and peered through a hole. " Barbers are shaving the heads of our women. We will teach him," they

fig. 40. Fox and crocodile

said. "Let me explain" the rich man pleaded "it is not my doing . . . lord Mahādeva did it." But the people gave him a sound beating. The rich man got what he deserved.

Animal Wisdom Stories

Folk wisdom and common sense are often expressed through animal stories.

FOX AND CROCODILE

A fox and a crocodile were acquaintances but not good friends. The fox did not trust the crocodile. The crocodile was always waiting for an opportunity to eat him up.

The crocodile knew that the fox loved to eat the juicy berries of a tree that grew upstream. "I will make two heaps, one of ripe berries and other of green berries and lie hidden under the heap of ripe berries. He is bound to fall into my trap." When the fox came he said, "I always eat the ripe berries.

Today I feel like eating green ones" The crocodile was disappointed.

The next day he lay very still under the water, not too far away from the edge of the stream. "He is sure to step in to drink after his feast. I get him then." The fox came again but being afraid of water and crocodile he perched himself carefully on the gnarled roots of a tree and barely dipped his nose into the shallow water as he drank. Suddenly his foot slipped and he slid far out, right into the mouth of the crocodile. The cunning fox thought fast, "That is not my foot, it is the foot of the tree you silly crocodile." He called out. The crocodile could not resist replying, "you think you are smart, don't you?" he said, opening his mouth and the fox escaped once more.

The next day the cunning fox ran straight to Mahādeva, the Great God. "You must protect me. It is no longer safe for me to go eating berries. May I have some food." The God pointed to a spot not far away. "You will find some

fig. 41. Buffalo and orphan

rounds of wheat bread under those dry cow-dung cakes." The fox removed the cow-dung cakes to get wheat bread. As he opened his mouth to eat, he was stung by a scorpion and died.

All the carefully laid plans of the crocodile to kill the fox had failed. But when the time came for him to die even a Mahādev could not save the cunning fox.

BUFFALO AND ORPHAN

An orphan boy came to a village. A farmer who had many buffaloes took him home. The boy began to look after the buffaloes driving to pasture every day. The buffaloes thrived but the boy was hungry, for the farmer starved him. A kind buffalo noticed this and said to the boy, "hold out a cup made of leaves to my mouth and you shall have a full meal every day." The farmer was curious about the boy's increasing good health and sent his daughter out with the buffaloes. The unsuspecting boy held out two leaf bowls, one for the girl and one for himself. The girl came back and reported to her father about the magic buffalo.

The buffalo realized that the farmer would soon sell him off at a huge price. He warned the boy, " When he comes to take me, hang on to my tail. As they chase me we will escape together." And finally they ran away.

Every night as the boy played on his flute, seven heavenly damsels, invisible to the boy, but clearly seen by the buffalo, would dance to his music. The buffalo told the boy about the seven heavenly sisters. "You will not see them. But tonight, stop playing and ask for the hand of the youngest sister in marriage. They will show you a wooden doll and a dog, expecting you to choose the doll. Choose the dog instead." The boy did as he was told. The buffalo ordered, "Burn the hair off the dog." As the boy obeyed, the skin burnt away leaving a beautiful young girl.

ANT AND FOX

The fox had challenged and defeated all the other animals, even the tiger, in a race. This news spread fast in the forest. He would soon be declared the

fig. 42. Ant and fox

fig. 43. Old woman and the tiger

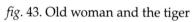

fastest runner at a gathering. As the animals collected, the fox fluffed himself out, put his snout up in the air and swished his tail about. Success had filled him with pride.

A humble ant then spoke up, "You haven't raced me yet. I am sure I can defeat you." As the other animals gasped with surprise, the fox accepted the challenge. They started off. The ant called out, "One moment you will see me behind you and even as you turn round, I will be there before you."

It was as the ant had said. All along his path, the fox would be followed by the ant one moment and be left behind the next. As he finished, tired, and panting, he saw the ant just ahead, craving calmly to victory. "You are cunning" said the ant. "But we ants are clever too. It was never the same ant. We ants are everywhere, you foolish fox."

OLD WOMAN AND THE TIGER

An old man and woman lived in a hut in a forest. A tiger used to pass by, waiting for an opportunity to attack them. The old man called out to the tiger one day, "There is no food for you here. Why do you come everyday?" "Yes, there is food for me. I am planning to kill you both and eat you" said the tiger.

The old man had to think fast. "You can have us. But let us finish threshing this grain first. Could you bring some of your friends along with you?" The tiger came with his friends. And they began to thresh the grain. The old woman had gained time. She had secretly prepared chains. She bound the tigers down one by one and branded them with hot irons. But they all got away. Only one of them died.

The animals in the forest collected for the dead tiger's rites. A fox sat on a grinding stone and his tail hung down through a hole in it. The old man lay hidden below this stone. He pulled at the fox's tail. As the fox started writhing and howling, the animals ran away saying, "The old man is God himself. He can cast spells on us." And the old couples were troubled no more by the wild animals in the jungle.

GREEDY TIGER

A hare, a deer, a tortoise, a fox and a giant lizard were out looking for a place to stay. A tiger on the prowl happened to meet them. "You can all come home with me. I live in a large cave. There is room for all of us." The animals followed the tiger to his cave. No sooner had they entered than the tiger growled and said, "Now you are trapped. I am going to eat one by one." The hare, who had sharp ears had slipped out even as the tiger's friendly voice changed to a growl. The tiger went chasing after him and this gave the others the chance to escape.

All but the tortoise. "I'll never be able to get away before the tiger returns," he moaned. The tiger, having lost the other animals, soon came back. He smacked his lips hungrily and said, "At least you are still here." The tortoise looked up and said, "I know I can't escape death, but feel my shell. It

fig. 44. Greedy Tiger

is so hard it will crack your teeth. You'll have to throw me into a stream and leave me soaking for a while. I'll be tasty morsel then." The tiger fell for the tortoise's story. He waited for the tortoise to swim back and then realized that he had been tricked once more. The tortoise too had gone away.

IV. Contemporary Warli Paintings

Warli paintings are made out in thousands by a large class of Warli artists. The variety of themes and subjects is innumerable. Despite simple living, their awareness of the supreme reality, the benevolent god and all that he does are manifested in very many paintings. There is conceptual depth, presentation of forces much beyond us that also look after us. Warlis are afraid to displease gods and therefore have woven round a large number of tales and myths to perpetuate the feeling that the benevolent God is always looking after you in many forms. He is invoked on all occasions.

Warli paintings in themselves are a combination of stories, myths, realities, religion, entertainment, humour etc. They contain far deeper meaning than what they show on surface. There is multiplicity of day-to-day activities that figure in the paintings. The dominant themes are-harvesting time, the decorations in the *maṇḍap* and the *maṇḍala*, fishing, community eating, marriage with all preparations and elaborate rituals. Among rituals the marriage rituals are most important. For example, the groom arrives on the shoulders of two strong men up to the bride's place. His feet should not touch ground lest evil spirits attack them. Rice plays an important role in wedding rituals. The Warlis dance to the tune of the *tarpa* until the puja of the tiger god. Dance and music abound in Warli art.

Reverence exists for ancestors, for elements of nature such as sun, moon, reverence for vegetation and very many more. The feeling of veneration is strengthened again and again through rituals and prolonged celebrations connected with numerous occasions — harvesting, marriage, death, birth etc. Rituals and festivities lend colour, meaning and even significance to life.

Legend, tradition, folklore, abound in Warli art. They remind one of Aesop's Tales from ancient Greece. Some of them are supernatural, eerie, mystical yet carry a lesson or a moral all pointing to an allegory. There is a full awareness of the supernatural and a deep trust in the benevolent nature of God.

The paintings are a visual delight. The base shape of two triangles joined at the vertex, sometimes with a little bent, are used in an artistic manner to make human and animal figures. Men may be standing erect, in a dancing pose created with a little bent, men climbing a tree, driving an animal-drawn cart or even a car with its lights on, a man loading a bus with luggage on to the roof, a woman cooking with a ladle in her hand, woman threshing to get rice, lighting a cracker at Diwali, a cow eating hay, women drawing water from a pond, etc. are also seen.

Mass dancing in a circular or coiled formation to the beat of a *tarpa* player who stands in the centre is a common theme. This is in absolute harmony with Warlis' basic belief of thanking God for all that he has given to mankind. There is a newly married couple on a horse with all three formed from the basic triangle shape. The women are singled out with a tuft behind their head. Triangles are basic for all *maṇḍala* and motif .figures too. And to top it all, a dark single colour background with figures drawn in absolute white with rice powder, is enchanting. The background colours include light and dark green, light and dark violet, geru, and brown.

Warli Life in Activities

Warli's village life

fig. 45

fig. 46

fig. 47

fig. 48

fig. 49

Warli Life in Activities

Warli's village life

fig. 50

fig. 51

Warli's village life

fig. 52

fig. 53   *fig.* 54

Warli Life in Activities

Warli's village life

fig. 55

fig. 56   *fig.* 57

Warli Life in Activities

Warli's village life

fig. 58

fig. 59

fig. 60

fig. 61

Warli Life in Activities

Warli's village life

fig. 62

fig. 63

fig. 64

Warli Life in Activities

Warli's village life

fig. 65

fig. 66

fig. 67

fig. 68

Warli Life in Activities

Warli People

fig. 69

fig. 70

fig. 71

fig. 72

Warli Life in Activities

Warli People

fig. 73

fig. 75

fig. 74

Warli Life in Activities

Warli People

fig. 76

fig. 77

fig. 78

Warli Life in Activities

Warli Dance

fig. 79

fig. 80

Warli Life in Activities

Warli Dance

fig. 81

fig. 82

Warli Life in Activities

Warli Life in Activities
Warli Dance

fig. 83

fig. 84

Warli Life in Activities

Marriage Rituals

fig. 85

fig. 86   *fig.* 87

Warli Life in Activities

Marriage Rituals

fig. 88

fig. 89

fig. 90

Warli Life in Activities

Marriage Rituals

fig. 91

fig. 92

Warli Life in Activities

Auspicious Motifs

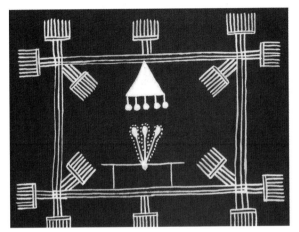

fig. 93

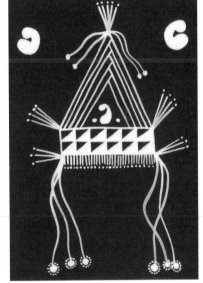

fig. 94

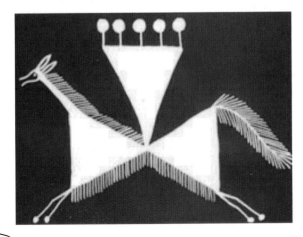

fig. 95

Other Rituals

Bāghadeva

fig. 96

fig. 97

Other Rituals

Goddess Pālaghāṭ

fig. 98

Other Rituals

Village Deity and Marrige Chauk

fig. 99

fig. 100

Other Rituals

Holī Festivities

fig. 101

fig. 102

Auspicious Motifs

fig. 103

fig. 104

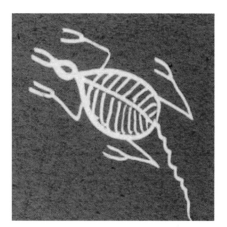

fig. 105

fig. 106

fig. 107

Auspicious Motifs

fig. 108

fig. 109

fig. 110

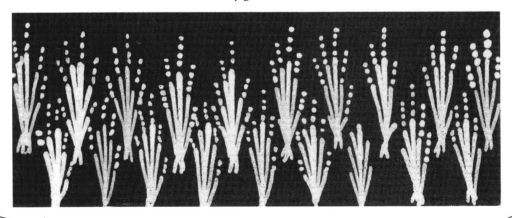

Conclusion

Help it Stay on the Time Continuum

Art of drawing was created by the primitive man who, by chance, discovered it by making images on sand. Once discovered, the tradition of creativeness continued through generations from rock shelters to tribal art, from tribal art to settled agricultural communities and from there to village folk and traditional art. Thereafter, emerged the classical arts and crafts of India. Art in all its dimensions — tribal, rock, folk. and classical — ancient and contemporary — is today a well established discipline the world over.

Normally individuals and society perceive the universe to appear as a continuous process of events within the framework of time-space coordinates. This is the European way of thinking and is sought to be adopted in other parts of the world. These events are then located and expressed within specific cultural historical context. But there is tremendous neglect in understanding indigenous traditions, their theoretical models and regional or temporal distributions. Today it is felt important to study in detail this aspect of cultural heritage.

Many tribes have managed to live in isolation without much contact with the outside world. There is a positive side to this. This has preserved in remote jungles, original rituals, magic and collective tribal consciousness. Most tribal customs and rituals existed centuries before the spread of Hindu and Vedic influence. These are recorded by Warlis in memory, oral convention and otherwise, that forms the tradition of events and situations.

Ancient rock paintings and carving in Bhimbhedka and Raisen in Madhya Pradesh (India), are quite close to such tribal paintings of Warlis. This art thus seems to have its roots in the rock shelters of ancestors. The essence of primitive art was thus not lost. It is evident in spirited expressions in tribal arts of India especially in Warli's art which in itself is a rich and unbroken tradition spanning thousands of years.

World over, tribals usually decorate their surroundings. There is an intrinsic desire to keep their home and surroundings clean and embellished with art. A tribal way of life symbolizes the early strata in the evolution of human culture. Tribal people provide us with a unique opportunity to see how have humans related to the world around them from earliest times. Their imaginative faculties and states of emotion are rich and complex. Their myths and customs emerge from the store of the community's collective mind and involve extensive use of animal, plants, gods, demons and other elements of nature. Warlis are well aware of modern happenings too and show them in their art.

Tribal artist draws upon his ancient memories and instinct, on images evoked by songs and dances, on festivals and rituals, and the environment. Dances of spring, of budding trees, of the meeting of lovers, and the poise and abandon, form an important repertoire in the tribal vocabulary. Couple entwined in each other's arms move with a swaying movement to the beat of the drums setting into motion the magical forces of nature. There is joy in the stomping of the feet and the rhythmic chanting of songs. Warlis like to dance to the beat of drums and sound of pipes. Nothing is static here.

The tree, human figure, birds fighting — everything happening in life is presented in Warli art in simple white strokes. From walls and floor, the Adivasi has graduated to paper and canvas to cater to the market for decorative art. Yet, he retains the energetic strokes and the paper comes alive with light and movement. More than this, the Warli art shows their cosmic view, ability to be in touch with the supernatural and their understanding of the mystic existence of life beyond. It is in this sense that ethnology, myths, religious beliefs and other traditions throw an alternative way of viewing their culture through art.

Many Warli paintings resemble primitive cave paintings in their economic use of concepts with display of simplicity. For instance, the human form consists of just two triangles, one pointing downwards and one pointing upwards with small strokes of the brush to form limbs. All activities of daily life including celebrations, cooking, threshing, hunting and many others are fully expressed through the Warli's simple human form. Innumerable well-knit *mandalas* born out of their knowledge of the earth and the vegetation around are a significant part of Warli art. The magic, power and the virility inherited from ancient rock drawings and etchings of their ancestors are reflected in Warli pictographs of today. Here is a true reflection of preservation of ancient art.

Creation, supernatural happenings as well as social events are the themes painted. Warli art shows a unique relationship among man, tree, bird, and fish and animals, flora and fauna — all that comprise the whole universe. Drawings are always in white lines capturing everyday life scenes, gods and goddesses, nature as perceived by them, men and women and animals. Changes occurring with the march of time are also observed. Images of trains with puffing engines, motor cars, bullock carts, are all absorbed and translated into the tribal idiom. A number of events will be shown in a single picture to make a story. The vastness of space has shrunk into a small canvas. But there is a flip side. The old traditions are fast vanishing. Because of poverty Warlis are becoming bonded labour, tilling their master's land. Some innocent tribals have been forced to abandon their tribal values and take to commercial avocations. Yet, what makes a person wonder is the tenacity of the artist, his patience and skill in keeping this art buoyant *till now* despite numerous commercial attractions elsewhere. And to top it all, the art has preserved its originality yet has encompassed within it all that is going on in today's world — the car, cycle, automobile etc. But a stage has come that a strong initiative from the society is called for to find ways and means to protect the art from vanishing and getting lost for ever as has already happened in the Euro-American context.

We have to do all we can to save this art from falling off from the pathway of the time continuum.

Glossary

ai	mother
Āśvini	month of October
ba-siṅga	headdress worn by bridegroom
bhagata	priest
Bāghadeva	tiger god
bhagatahood	training of priest
bovana	circular rangoli
chauka	auspicious square space
Cheda god	ancestor's god
ḍamarū	small drum
Dhantari	earth goddess
Gavatari	mother cow
geru	red mud
kamdi	a kind of dance
Kansari	corn goddess
khaḍga	sword
kṣetrapāla	gods of the region
kṣetra	region
Māgha	month of September
Phālguna	month of March
Pālaghāṭ	goddess of tree and plants
Pānadeva	god of vegetation
pānapātra	wine vessel
Himai	mountain's mother
suvasini	married women

savani	field goddess
sarpañca	village chief
sindūra	red stone powder
tandula	rice
tarpa	musical pipe
triśula	spear
ukhala	whole
Vaiśākha	month of May
*vīra*s	ancestor's gods

Bibliography

Beir, Ulli, *Soma Mase and Other Warli Painters*, Port Morseby, 1977.

Benjamin, Walter, *Illustrations*, New York, 1988.

Bhattacharya, N.N., *Indian Mother Goddess*, Calcutta, 1971.

Briffault, R., *The Mother: A Study of Origin of Sentiments and Infatuations*, vols. I-III, London, 1927.

Coomarswamy, A.K., *The Transformation of Nature in Art*, New York, 1956.

Dalmia, Yashodara, *The Painted World of Warlis*, New Delhi, 1988.

Elvin, Verrier, *The Religion of an Indian Tribe*, Bombay, 1955.

Enthoven, R.E., *Tribes and Castes of Bombay Presidency*, vol. 1, Bombay, 1920

Ghategi, A.N., *Warli of Thane: A Survey of Marathi Dialects*, VII, Bombay.

Jain, Jyotindra, *Painted Myths of Creation: Art and Rituals of an Indian Tribe*, New Delhi, 1984.

Jaykar, Pupul, *The Earthern Drum : An Introduction to the Ritual Art in India*, New Delhi, 1981.

Kramrisch, Stella, *Unknown India : Rural Art in Tribe and Village*, Philadelphia, 1968.

Naik, T.B., *The Bhils : A Study*, Delhi, 1956.

Narayan Rao, M.V., "Madhubani and Warli Folk Paintings", *Marg*, 19.

Parulekar, Godavari, *Adivasi's Revolt : The story of Warli Peasants in Struggle*, Bombay, 1945.

Phare, R.C., *Lajja Gauri*, Pune, 1978.

Sabavala, Radhika, "Warlis", *Marg*, vol. XXXIV, no. 4, pp. 101-02.

Save, K.J., *The Warlis*, Bombay, 1945.

Upadhayay, Ashok, "Peasantisation of Adivasis in Thane District", *Economic and Political Weekly*, Bombay, 1980

Wakankar, Vishnu, *Robert Brooks Stone Age Paintings in India*, Bombay, 1976.

Wilson, John, *Aborginal Tribe of Bombay Presidency*, Bombay, 1876.

————, *Cave Temples and Other Ancient Remains of Westrn India*, Bombay, 1850

Zimmer, *Myths and Symbols in Indian Arts and Civilisation*, New York, 1946.

Index

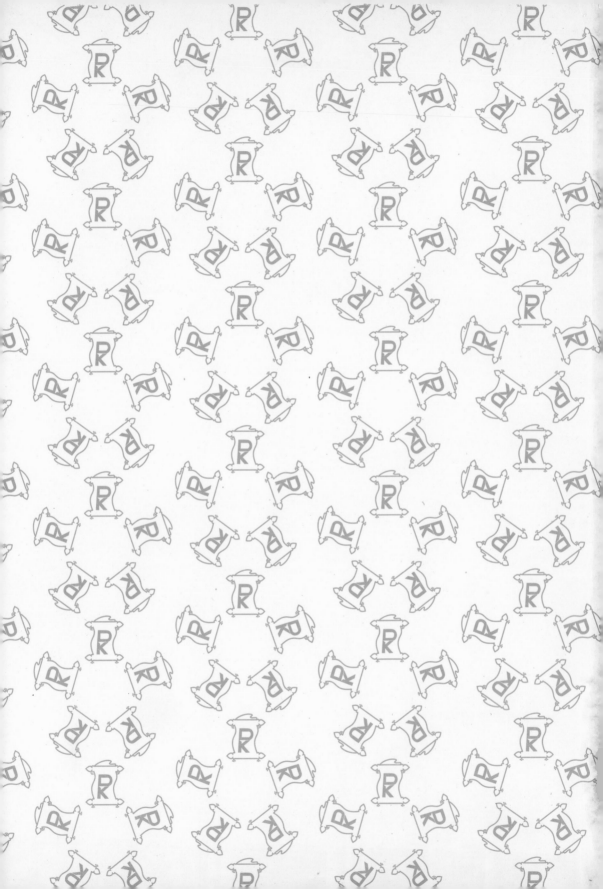